Raindrops

Written by Jon Madian
Illustrated by Carol Schwartz

MONDO

Raindrops. Plop! Plop!

Fill the puddle. Plop! Plop!

Fill the stream. Plop! Plop!

Fill the lake. Plop! Plop!

Fill the river. Plop! Plop!

Fill the sea. Plop! Plop!

Raindrops, fill the glass. Plop! Plop!